All My Ghosts Are Here

poems by

John Smith

Finishing Line Press
Georgetown, Kentucky

All My Ghosts Are Here

ACKNOWLEDGMENTS

Berfrois: "Leftovers"; "Great Village"
Paterson Literary Review: "Would Be Sam"
Ragazine: "That Grackle"
Shotglass Journal: "Ash Wednesday"; "Blue Note"
Slant: "Emphysema"
Smartish Pace: "It's Okay"
Spillway: "Capsula Mundi"
US1: "Chopping Wood"

Publisher: Leah Huete de Maines
Editor: Christen Kincaid
Cover Art: Joe Strasser
Photo of Cover Art: Scott Peterson, Shy Hound Photography
Author Photo: Catherine Lent
Cover Design: Elizabeth Maines McCleavy

Order online: www.finishinglinepress.com
            also available on amazon.com

Author inquiries and mail orders:
Finishing Line Press
P. O. Box 1626
Georgetown, Kentucky 40324
U. S. A.

Table of Contents

VLADIMIR: *What do they say?*
ESTRAGON: *They talk about their lives.*
VLADIMIR: *To have lived is not enough for them.*
ESTRAGON: *They have to talk about it.*

~Samuel Becket, Waiting for Godot

All My Ghosts Are Here

1
Early spring, under a hammered-nickel bowl of sky,
a woman sets a field of iris beds on fire.
Shad run, lilacs bloom.
Bullfrogs pop like pickle jar lids in muddy ponds
while an orb-weaver weaves a sticky trampoline
there is no bouncing back from.
A dead mouse quakes in the grass
like a fur pouch of jumping beans.
Bees buzz in and out of its mouth.
My body is riddled with catacombs.

2
We read our planet's strata as if they are pages of a book
about what we used to know.

What the body needs sucks us into ourselves
like quicksand, weighs us down.

Every year, I fall behind weeding my way out of August.

3
You can't convince a stone that believes it's a bird
it doesn't have wings.

I want to explode like a touch-me-not
and hurl seed in every direction
instead of shrapnel.

4
Behold: a crop circle doughnut
furrowed by a four-wheeler.

Nobody likes a bird that shits its own nest.

Forget starlings, Japanese stilt grass,
emerald ash borer, and mile-a-minute vine,
we are the most invasive species on the planet.

5

The old ones worshipped the moon instead of the sun
because they didn't need light during the day.
We worship a light we do not see.

Swaying like a metronome on an otherwise motionless
catalpa tree, the single limb could be waving.
What harm in me waving back?
Isn't the case for objectivity subjective?

I have been talking to deer for years.

6

Down by the river towers a sycamore so thick
I can't reach my arms even halfway around it.

Wind-scattered swarms of gnats
re-group like bubbles rising
in flutes of champagne.

An Indian pipe pokes its periscope up
from the damp forest floor,
then hangs its head low
like the spirit of a rose.

I spy a spotted lantern fly
in the tree of heaven.

7

Once God was one; then, one god among many.
Now, God is dead, and this is what it is
as I am that I am, who knows of red trillium
in woods above Twelfth Street and bloodroot
scattered along the rail trail beyond.

8

Nobody hears the wind's score beforehand
or knows what's on in the offing.
Besides, an afterlife won't save us.
Not even a virtual one.

Adam and Eve's expulsion
from the Garden of Eden
isn't myth or parable.
It's prophecy.

9
Consider our species to be supermarket employees
training customers how to use the new
self-check-out registers
that will replace them.
Consider the singularity to be a blessing;
our extinction, an evolutionary necessity.

10
If there is an afterlife, let it be this again,
this and everything that's missing.

That there be love all the same but more of it.

That there be joy in each other
and compassion for everything living.

That cooperation
and the betterment of all beings
be the rule of thumb,
not competition.

Though I imagine what it might be
to be beyond my ken.
Or nothing. The unknowing.
But if there is something, that it be here.
All my ghosts are here.

Leftovers

One day I will be nothing but what I've left behind:
a roomful of poetry books boxed for yard sale or
library donation including a signed copy of *Guide
to the Underworld* by Gunnar Ekelof and a limited,
cloth-bound edition of *The Naming of the Beasts*
by Gerry Stern that I stole from Somerset County
College. A striped coffee mug of my mother's.
Her mother's bundt pan. Her father's Captain badge
from the Newark Fire Department. My father's painting
of the Great Swamp. Birthday cards from daughters.
A dusty shoe box of home videos I never converted
to digital. A handful of poems for my wife. The Tinker,
my Swiss Army knife. My last will and testament split
and spent; the house, painted three times over,
paid for and on the market. My garden, a lawn.
That photograph of me leaning on the shovel
between tomatoes and basil hanging on a wall
or kneeling on a dresser in my daughters' homes.
Johnny's stuffed hot peppers! Old Facebook posts.
Instagram shots. Involuntary paintings.
The patchwork quilt of stories that my children tell
about me worn thin, until, within three generations,
I will be a chiseled name and two dates on stone,
a twig on a family tree. Nothing left of me
but a genetic trait: a great-granddaughter's cat allergy
or her brother's nail-biting habit. I understand the terms
of the lease. I am not looking to live forever, but to pass on
a bit more than just DNA. To be recycled, if you will,
transplanted, or grafted. I want my eyes to open the blinds
for someone on a seaside sunrise or their hand-shaped
landscape of a loved one's face. I'd have my hands play tag
and catch fireflies, again. For my skin to dress a burn victim
is all the afterlife I'm asking. It beats being ashes
dumped in the Great Swamp or scattered off the coast
of Point Pleasant. Who knows, one spring my lungs might fill
with lilac while a lover waits outside in the dark
for a bedroom light to blink twice. Maybe one sunny day

a pregnant woman in a city park will fend off bullies
who threaten to beat a boy sitting on a bench
for painting his fingernails red, the blood pumping
through her righteous veins by my second-hand heart,
a vital part of me given to live and let live again.

Chopping Wood

The night our daughter curled up on her bed like a cannonball
and exploded into a pool of tears was the night I decided to teach her
about splitting wood. Not just how to set the log on end in the center
of the tree-stump, plant her feet, grip the ax with one hand at the base,
steady it halfway up the shaft with the other, take aim, and swing
hard enough to drive the blade all the way through, into the stump,
but also, that it is less about strength than the speed of confidence.
Not to mention there is great venting to be had. The next day,
I placed a log on the chopping block and said, this wood is you
and him, and the axe head, all the reasons for the split.
You have to keep repeating it, keep slamming into the wood,
cleaving it in two, piece after piece, until there is relief in the rhythm
and reward when you see your efforts stack up. The evening fire,
a little brighter for all your hard work. We put the ax back in the shed
and loaded the wheelbarrow with firewood. As we headed to the house,
she asked how long it took me to stop drinking. Every day of it, I said.

For the Good People at IGA

When the cashier we are most grateful for
shows up to duty at the only grocery store still open,
her braces don't make her look as young
as they did before. The ankh tattoo on her neck
appears less abrasive, a badge of courage, even,
for manning the cash register during a pandemic,
certainly, reason enough to call attention to
the sexism inherent in language like "manning"
to begin with and reconsider what we mean by
menial labor and what we value as essential
and worthy of so much more than minimum wage.

Would Be Sam

Stella would be Sam, change her name,
trade "star" for "the name of god," as far
as meaning goes; and as far as her family
is concerned, swap her great-grandmother's
lineage for something more gender-ambiguous.
And I get the Adam/Madam name game,
the sexist bullshit labeling is, and the gender-
bending, gender-neutral emergency of her current
state of being. I am all about fluidity.
But it was Stella's placenta we buried,
planted a cherry tree. Stella posed
for fourteen springs beneath the blossoms,
both growing out of reach. And now she
who spent the past fourteen years defining who
Stella is is telling me Stella is Sam.
I went along with a rainbow-stained pixie,
the buzz cut, black pants tight as spray paint
and slashed to shreds, but I can't keep up
with The LGBTQIA acronym anymore.
It's like trying to juggle the alphabet.
I believe a rose by any other name...
but I am slow and forgetful and, admittedly,
lazy and resistant. Not that I care if she steps out
from behind the curtain and refuses to play
a socially-constructed character; assumes,
instead, a role of her own making
with a non-binary handshake
as long as she still has the same hug
and kiss for me, who swaddled her in his arms
and twirled around the hospital room
in a blue gown like a swooning Sufi
singing, *I Could Have Danced All Night*
the first morning of her life.
She is still the nervous person I sit with
three times a year while she stares down the needle
at her vein without flinching, determined
not to wince when the nurse breaks skin,

draws blood. Blood of my blood and her mother's
but her own being. A star in a galaxy of stars,
orbiting by this rotation as Sam,
soon to be followed, no doubt, by pronouns
streaking past like meteorites, and with them,
more confounding agreements, more blossoms
beyond my backward and clumsy reach.

Even This

Erratically flapping in zig-
zag flight, a
brown winged thing
swooped down
on the creek
less like a sparrow
or wren than
a sphinx moth
skimming the surface
for a drink, then
lifting,
flew over our heads.
High-noon sun
backlit scalloped wings,
translucent pink body,
no tail—a bat!—
thrashing in the cold breath
of February,
and we kissed
at such a rare sighting,
though we
would kiss at anything.

It's Okay

~a poem for two voices

It's okay, it's okay, I say.
The doe's ears twitch,
but it doesn't move,
tilts its head
as if wondering
whether or not to run.
Both eyes on me
for the answer.
It's okay, I nod,
show my hands.
The deer snorts twice,
shakes its head,
coaxing me
more than disagreeing
or, for all I know,
trying to comfort *me.*
I'm within a dozen feet
when its knees bend,
shoulders shift.
The doe leans back
on hind legs
and rears a bit
then turns and steps
into the woods,
ambles down a slope
and stops,
looks back,
her eyes dark
and distant planets.

It's okay, it's okay, I say,
as I sit beside my mother
and wrap an arm
around her shoulders,
frail as bird wings.
Slumped
on the edge of her bed,
her entire body
curls into itself.
She is shriveling.
Her head hangs low.
She calls me Paul
but knows I'm John.
I can tell
by the way she says,
I'm sorry.
50 years later
and I have no doubt
what she is talking about.
It's okay, I say.
I lower my head
and look up
into her eyes: no tears
but she is crying.
That's long forgiven.
Let it go, I say.
Okay? She nods,
her eyes dark
and distant planets.

Margaret's Garden Hands

Margaret's garden hands are dark,
mud-caked, bordered by lighter,
dried dirt, the pit of her palms
peeking through. They look like
blotchy prints of brown paint
a child pressed on a paper plate
or relief maps, the topography
of a life lived as close to earth
as a life can get this side of it.
But my sister's hands aren't prints
or raised maps. They're cultivators,
as were our father's, small
but strong and no strangers
to bare fistfuls of soil or fingernails
cracked and grouted; in fact,
first-hand familiar with the grip
and rip of weeds uprooted,
a clingy ball of earth, the weighty
shaking loose, and stubborn worms
that won't let go, even with
part of them writhing on the
ground beneath. Years ago,
among unripe tomato plants
and the warm, licorice scent
of basil, sweet as memory itself,
Margaret's hands were first
to touch our father lying
on his back in the garden,
life outgrown him. See how she
washes them now, one toughened
hand at a time, with the green
garden hose in the other.

Ghost of a Landmark

Everything has an afterlife
as long as someone
remembers it,

even landmarks that know nothing
of their place in the heart
of a memory.

Landmarks long since
disappeared from their posts
exist as ghosts

as long as they haunt someone.
A few years back before a smokestack
at an abandoned factory

alongside of a medical center
was finally imploded,
the daughter of a doctor

who worked at the clinic
trespassed with friends
through a gap

in the factory's chain-link fence
and climbed a rusty ladder of rungs
staple-stitched up the stack's side

to look down on the world,
but the last rung broke
and the daughter fell.

She was pronounced dead on arrival
at the hospital. For years
the doctor worked in the shadow

of that smokestack clocking the hours,
pointing a stiff finger at god, the reckless
moon and drunken stars, blaming them

for each cloudy day since,
until the days passed it by unnoticed.
Most of them, anyway.

When the stack collapsed,
a weight lifted from the doctor
and settled in at the same time.

The ghost of her daughter
drifted off with the smoke
from the implosion,

but after the smoke cleared
and the rubble was trucked off to a dump,
the empty space got lonely.

So, the doctor began reassembling
the smokestack, brick by brick,
as she walked past or looked out

on the vacant lot from work, even
the rusty rungs, right up to the moment
before the last rung let go

when her daughter looked down
triumphantly on street lights
shimmering like stars at her feet.

Cooper's Hawk

Mid-winter one year,
my bird feeder quieted,
abruptly abandoned.
I looked up from
doing dishes
out the kitchen window
to backyard, tree-top
lookout spots
and saw a Coopers hawk
perched on a branch
just as it dive-bombed
the congregation
of dark-eyed juncos
and white-throated sparrows
huddled ravenously
around spilled seed.
Like a rock dropped
in a puddle, its descent
sent them splashing
in every direction.
Then the raptor
bounced off the ground
and flew straight
at the window I was in
but banked,
just before the glass,
seeing me inside
or seeing another bird
in its own reflection
playing chicken head-on.
Though it scaled
a cliff of air
and vanished
before I knew
what I saw,
the black and white
blur of a junco

clutched in talons
underbelly
flashing by and gone
has stayed with me still.

Brown Sugar

If I button a cuff of the floral-print blouse
that a nurse dressed her in
to distract her from fidgeting
with the hospital gown snaps,
my mother allows me to feed her a spoonful
of oatmeal sprinkled with brown sugar
I brought from home.
Only white sugar where she is.
Then my mother unbuttons the sleeve cuff,
folds it over, and demands, *Button it.*
But I insist, *Only if you eat another spoonful.*
Resentfully, she surrenders.
The unbuttoning is everything.
Her false teeth float in a Styrofoam cup
on the nightstand while she sucks the spoon,
her mouth collapsed like a sinkhole
in her face. Thin skin shrunk skull-tight,
swollen purple-veins throb
at her temples. Her body
her only house now, and the eyes
light up for brown sugar when I visit.

Ash Wednesday

for Peter Mantell

I think I know what the pastor of the church across the street was thinking
as he repaired the life-size cross to be erected for Lent.
He wasn't worried about raising it upright in a muddy spring lawn,
nor was he concerned with draping a purple cloth in front of the post's neck
and over the back of both shoulders of the crossbar like a loose scarf,
or looping the material like a snake drooping from both out-stretched arms.
He didn't anticipate the Friday when he would switch purple cloth for black
or the following Sunday when he would trade in black for white,
wasn't focused on redemption as he drove a six-inch nail
into the beams' intersection, wobbly since last spring.
Though he said nothing, his thoughts rang out with every dull clang.
He was thinking about the hammer in his hand, how it fitted the hand
of someone long ago, as I was thinking how it fit my hand, too.

Capsula Mundi

When I first heard
of *capsula mundi*
world capsules
egg-shaped burial pods
made of biodegradable starch
planted in cemeteries
instead of caskets
and seeded
so that the body inside
fertilizes a tree
and funeral plots
become starter beds
from which the dead
rise as woods
and convert a graveyard
into a forest
I wanted to be sown
to nourish a sycamore
by a river
or a willow
but not for the weeping
rather the breeze
through my hair
or a birch tree
for the un-peeling
like pages of a book
opened by fire
anything other
than boxed in a casket
I would rather
be left out in the open
and torn apart by vultures
I am not afraid to be feed
or ashes scattered
on wind and wave
but to be part of a forest
would be marvelous

maybe a maple
with strong limbs
for climbing
and a green head of hair
full of whirligigs.

Casino Pier

Lucky Leo me tonight.
My heart's a carousel
of hand-carved and gilded horses.
Let me walk the boards again
like the tourist that I am
along a strip of neon lights,
thin slices of ocean strobing by
between the planks beneath my feet,
my sister skipping at my side,
a roller coaster in her eyes,
all Four Seasons singing
at the Chatterbox.
Let the arcade gamblers
lay down their last dimes
on MOM or 7 or the ace of spades
and spin the big wheel for the stars
or a color TV. Those prizes
don't mean anything to me
anymore. I know the waves
breaking against Casino Pier
are never the same waves.
Still, let the moon be a quarter
in my pocket tonight.
I don't care if the Skee Ball machine
sticks out a short tongue of tickets
taunting me to try again.
I don't want the ceramic-skull
with-wire-rim-glasses ashtray
like I did when I was a teenager,
anyway. Just the Chinese handcuffs
to lock fingers with my sister.

Seaside Heights, NJ

Cicada Song

Here they come again, Brood X,
exoskeletons risen from underground,
scaling trees to scorched tips
until their backs split open
and white spirits
with cellophane wings
and fire-beady eyes
emerge by the billions.
Then their bodies blacken,
and the crying, as old as desire,
begins, an eerie whir and whining
like 10,000 stones ringing
as they skip across an icy pond
or the reverberations
of a flying saucer invasion
in a B-movie.
But this isn't science fiction.
This story is older than the myth
of a god's trick played on a mortal
promised immortality, poor Tithonus,
destined to live forever
but have his body keep aging
until he shrivels up,
no more than a squealing insect
begging to be released
from recurring resurrections
in the same blistering season,
the endless misery of summers
suffered through the ages,
relentlessly reborn into a world
in blazes, damned to cyclical
metamorphoses
that don't change anything.
Sick of climbing the same tree,
a slave to mating,
Sick of the shrill drill
and faceless urgency of rote sex,

the world inflamed.
Sick of burning, buried,
burning again.
Sick of pleading
but not being heard by deaf gods
or crazed human beings,
zealous fire in their eyes,
never listening, too busy
screaming at each other
in the streets of the inferno below.

Embraceable You

for Tara

Some spines are stacked
more like tiddlywinks
than bricks;
some backbones bowed,
butt to brain;
some lean left,
while others spiral
like a staircase
of dominoes;
some smile,
some grimace.
And then there are those
that bend like a river flows;
and so, my love,
your curvature goes.
But you should know
not a backbone among us
stands straight as an arrow,
and everybody
wears a brace.
Some people are born into one,
some saddled along the way.
Others suit themselves
without knowing it.
A brace can be a bandage
or medal,
a straightjacket
or shield.
Worn on the inside
or out.
It's up to you.
But wear it you will,
strapped, snapped,
buckled, buttoned,
zipped or Velcroed,
sun up and moon down.

A brace can be a shell,
my dear,
thick or thin.
Or a cocoon.
It's up to you,
my sweet embraceable you.

Emphysema

As if God
couldn't see
through him
my grandfather
a hard-drinking
heavy-smoking
hell-bound
fireman
suddenly
Catholic again
in the middle
of the night
at the foot
of their bed
alongside
his oxygen tank
on his knees
wheezing
eyes bulging
above a tight
plastic mask
crying
my grandmother said
when she woke
and found him
frantically
washing
her feet.

How Daffy Duck Got Me Through Catholic School

As a kid, I believed in the saving grace of animation
and woke up early every Saturday morning for silly cartoons
after a grueling week marching in a straight line
ascending in size to desks alphabetically arranged
where I was trained from 8 to 3 (with only a half-hour break
for tater tots and dodge ball) to swallow and regurgitate
whatever hash the nuns dished out about crusades
or seven deadly sins. I did as told, kept my hands folded
on my desktop that doubled as a bomb shelter roof
where I cowered during air raid drills, as if a fountain-pen-
riddled board of pine would save my Catholic ass
from being burned, ashes to ashes, by Atomic radiation,
or the Hail Marys nuns insisted we repeat doused the fear
of hell right then and there under a desktop in New Jersey.
My lips moved while I squatted, scrunched up, hands
pressed flat together, but I wasn't praying. I woo-hooed
as I ricocheted off walls, floor, and ceiling inside my head
the way Daffy Duck would, body stiff as a corpse. Defying
the laws of gravity and reason, I bounced right through
the classroom doorway, down the hall, and out of the building,
then sprung from the entire educated planet strung tight
as a trampoline, and shot like a rocket into the sky
where I floated on a cloud, unreachable and safe.

In the Hands of the Ocean

As we waded out of the ocean,
my mother would slap my hand away
if I reached for hers too soon or,
worse yet, unnecessarily. Only she knew
when was right and would signal,
with her fingers by splashing water
at my closest hand which had better
be ready to hold hers tight
but look loosely engaged
as we strolled from the backwash
side by side, me keeping lookout
for incoming waves.
Rarely looking back,
Mom focused one leg at a time
on firm but hurried footing
and alternately hand-paddled
as fast as she could for shore.
She had fallen alone a few years ago
on the way in, floundered in the surf,
pinned between breakers and backwash
until, as she told it, a young woman—
though my sister says the Good Samaritan
was our mother's age—helped her up.
Embarrassed more than frightened,
Mom shook the friendly hand off
as soon as she could with a quick
Thank you. I'm okay. Since then,
she would not go in or leave the water
unaided. But once, delivered safely
beyond the breakers and over her head,
she floated on her back so comfortably,
it looked as though she had fallen asleep.
With her body sagging below the surface,
her hands, toes, and face sparkled
as they bobbed, carefree, over waves
like five star points on a blue bed of night.
While I waited to escort her out,

I often thought of my tiny hands
pressed against her upturned palms
as I pushed off on my own
and of my daughter's hand reaching for mine
someday soon enough when I need it.

Joan of Arc

for Margaret Joan Smith

When I sat at her bedside
and dubbed her Joan of Arc,
my mother laughed it off
but spoke as if she were narrating
On the Waterfront meets
One Flew Over the Cuckoo's Nest
with a feminist twist.
She told me, for the third time,
that she was summoned
from solitaire and romance novels
to restore democracy
but captured before she got started,
imprisoned here in the hospital,
strapped down at night. *Greed
is the disease,* she shrieked,
*doctors in bed with drug companies
keep the dying alive at any price—
and it costs plenty!
They milk us of our savings
while underpaid nurses
do all the dirty work.*
Her plan: lead the nurses in a strike
to unionize caregivers worldwide.
And won't the media be surprised,
her eyes caught fire, *that a woman
did it! A retired teacher with arthritis
living in a country where Trump
is running for president—
can you believe it?* she glared at me,
dumbfounded. My mother,
who believed in unions, justice,
and equality right up until the end,
so far gone was she.

Last Loaf of Bread

What if I had the last loaf of bread on earth?
Would I share it freely? Or would that depend
on who was hungry and if they knew I had bread
to begin with? Would I slice it evenly
or turn the blade in my favor? Or theirs?
How big a loaf are we talking about, anyway?
Is it semolina or rye? Not white bread, I hope!
Or a five-pound organic brick with 10,000 grains
and a handful of mulch—although bulk and nutrition
might be key to survival. And isn't survival
what it's all about? And hardwired?
If it came down to the last loaf of bread
and starving to death, wouldn't I shift into id,
revert to the primitive, and would it, then,
really be up to me? Wouldn't I
be beside myself with hunger and panic
like someone drowning and claw
at the very lifeguard struggling to save me,
selfishly pull myself up on the desperate raft
of their sinking body for a mouthful of air?
Or can love be bread enough?
Would I swallow my own life to feed a loved one?
And if not, could I live with myself
having hid so much as a crumb? Also,
is there wine with this bread or what?

Rolling in the Dead

for Lauren

My daughter and I took River Road for the tiger lilies
and rapids, one curve so sharp we lost sight of a black sports car
in front of us, and when we rounded the bend,
I spotted something white flopping just off the shoulder
in the drainage ditch. A dog's been hit, I gasped,
U-turned, raced back, flashing my headlights at oncoming traffic.
Hurry, Daddy, hurry! Lauren pleaded from her car seat.
I cut across double yellow lines and skidded to a stop
on a grassy embankment. When I flung open my door,
a deadly odor gagged me, and I saw a white mop of a dog
squirming on its back, rubbing head, neck, and shoulders
against a maggot-covered possum rotting in the ditch.
Kicking at the air between us, I yelled, *Go home,*
scatted the dog away, watched it trudge off begrudgingly,
leering over a grimy shoulder as I turned to the horrified face
in the car window. I knew the dog would be back as soon as I left.
He had to come back. Just as I had to return to the car,
and ease my daughter's distress, blame wolves in dogs' ancestry
for their beastly ways, and later lie in bed turning the rancid
memory over in my head, rubbing up against the rotten truth,
anointing myself with the oily stench of what the living do to survive.

The Sound of Music

When I saw my daughter dressed as a nun
on stage, hands pressed together in prayer,
her back to a stone wall unrolled from the sky,
eyes fixed upward, a small lift in the upper lip
giving her smile a slightly wry twist,
I imagined her wondering what, if anything,
was up there or thinking, the curtains are dirty,
even the air clogged with dust or that row of lights
could unhinge and kill me.
Though those were my thoughts, no doubt,
more so than hers, my disgust, distrust, and fear,
my Catholic upbringing projected on the lighting,
a curtain opening on the cruel fist of injustice
knocking on my door in the guise of nuns—
penguins, we called them, starched habits
packing 18-inch rulers that struck at will
if we misspoke or misbehaved,
or simply weren't paying attention,
the sting still seething under years of dust
until my daughter sang,
How do you hold a moonbeam in your hand?
with her cupped hands reaching out from her heart
not to capture but to offer a safe place
to harbor moonlight, for a while,
as much as anyone can, one fascist or another
always pounding at the door.

Belated Apology

I want to apologize to my father
standing on the second step
looking down at me
in a wobbly-drunk boxing stance
glaring up at him
from the off-limits living room,
ready to punch it out,
slurring, *Come on; come on.*
I've seen the look on his face
in the mirror since then:
swollen red with hurt and anger,
about to burst into furious tears;
instead, he just turned
and slowly ascended
into the blinding hall light,
leaving me with my fists in the air
and my back to a room
of immaculate furniture
wrapped in plastic,
reserved for company.

Most Doleful

Bird of the slow waddle,
belly full of 10,000 seeds,
head bobbing fast
as a sewing machine.

Sleek, feathered gourd
wading through waves of grass
in no hurry to go anywhere
but where the grains are.

Wide-eyed, startled one
astonished by everything,
whose wings paddle briskly
against gravity

struggling to lift the soft weight
of its pear shape
even a short distance to safety
then cushion its descent.

Bird of the shoddy nest,
flimsy stick-work, eggs peeking
out underneath, too busy
brood-making to make neat.

Buddha's belly. Noah's
olive branch. Mohammed's
confidant. Aladdin's lamp
with wishes for mighty wings.

Paltry sacrifice at the altar
of voracious gods.
Meager meal on the table
of the ravenous poor.

Most doleful mourning dove
cooing on a branch
or telephone wire
contemplating the wall of air.

Lunaria

For the gardener who turned over the earth by hand
and turned into earth in turn,
who pick-axed, shoveled, wheel-barrowed, and railroad-tied
the backyard slope into terraces.
who uprooted rocks to build flower beds around dogwood
and cherry trees he transplanted from woods at the end of the street.
who planted lunaria and taught me how to peel back
the skin of the moon.
who lined our driveway with Belgian block he stole
from cul-de-sacs *encroaching on the Great Swamp!*
who kept a compost heap and freed tomatoes from cages
and stakes, let them ripen lying down un-insecticided
and fend for themselves against beetles and slugs.
who grew Egyptian onions, lovage, and sage.
who trimmed back pachysandra with the lawnmower.
The ancient Chinese, he said, *beat young plants with sticks*
to make them stronger.
whose live-forever was split and divided among his children
after his heart stopped on his back in the sour shade
of green tomatoes.
whose ashes we buried under his lace-leaf maple tree
in the yard that no longer belongs to us.
who danced at a wedding reception the last time I saw him
like there was no tomorrow.
Now that he hasn't any. Now that his children are his tomorrows
who would rather his voice rise from the yellow porch light
calling us in for the night,
who would kiss his stubbled cheek before going to sleep.

My Grandmother's Rose

Every summer during high school,
my grandmother packed a trunk,
left Brick City, and spent her vacation
in coal country, PA
where she met a farm boy
who taught her how to play the ukulele
and took her to a barn dance
with holes in the roof full of stars.
When she woke the following morning,
a rose redder than the sun
was sleeping on her windowsill.
Summer senior year, she returned home
and married a heavy-drinking fireman
who was a thorn in her side
until emphysema extinguished him.
Before dementia shuffled her past
like a deck of cards and she
could no longer tell hearts from clubs,
she would repeat the same few stories,
none of which mentioned my grandfather.
One was about how she pleaded
with my parents not to give me
my first haircut and saved a curl
when they did but lost it.
I would remind her that she gave it to me
when I was in my twenties
and that I still had it.
Once, I even brought the envelope
with me when I visited,
and she was so happy she cried.
Always, as I got up to leave,
Grandma would grab my arm and say,
Did I ever tell you...
and then came the story of the boy
with a ukulele, a roof full of stars,
and the window like a glass vase
holding on to a rose
as red as they come.

Passing through Jersey

If you're passing through Jersey,
stop in Shop-Rite or A&P
and pick up a pound of Taylor Ham,
pork roll, ground fat and pink flesh
compressed, molded and packed
in a small, tube-like sack
with red lettering. Look for the O
with a white cross in the middle.

At home, score, then peel
the burlap casing back from the loaf,
a marbleized capsule of pork,
sphinctered at both ends.

Thick or thin slice, notch
four times—like a Maltese cross
but rounded like a fireman's badge—
and fry.

You'll agree: God bless
John Taylor and God bless Trenton.
God bless and forgive all of New Jersey
for delivering the pig unapparent,
reconfigured, dissociated from slaughter,
transubstantiated, and presented,
via spatula, on breakfast plates
across the state or Kaiser rolls
with egg and cheese and ketchup
or wrapped in foil, incubating
under red hot lights
at any convenience store
from the back roads
to the clotted turnpike.

Buoy 2M

It was the summer of Corpse Cam,
livestream from the Brooklyn
Botanical Museum
featuring an orchid
the size of a whale's penis
blossoming
for the first time in a decade
unleashing a stench
like rotten fish
but sweet.
And there was a gathering
of blue-bottle flies
to fill their hairy vials
and thousands of photographers
documenting the flowering,
and the flower
like a long-necked bird
with inverted
umbrella-like wings unfolding
only craned from its shell
for a few days
before wilting.
The summer rain
clouded out
Perseid meteor showers.
The summer of ocean buoy 2M
off Manasquan Inlet
from *man-a-tah*
"stream-of-the-island-of squaws"
according to the Turtle People
who came before us.
The buoy that marks
our family's watery plot
where on our mother's birthday
my sister and I
scattered her ashes
like a cloud in the waves,

and they floated on the surface
then sank as she swam
to join her siblings
who had already sifted
through the salt water
back to the beginning.

Great Village

1

Some nights Elizabeth lay in bed
staring longingly through a skylight
in her blue ceiling, pretending
she was riding on a glass-bottom boat,
stars swimming past like slow fish.

Others, she aimed her flashlight at the glass,
blinked it off and on, and imagined
she was holed-up in a lighthouse
signaling stars sailing by
to rescue her from home.

2

Cowbells and books,
cast iron irons, skeleton keys,
and torchiere glass shades
all shelved inside her grandparents' house.

Flat on its back out back
with only T H E R carved in it
rests half a granite tombstone
under a crabapple tree.

A green, lichen-crusted arbor
leans over a garden
given up to weeds.

Beyond the barbed fence,
a dandelion field glows so bright yellow
it looks like the sun just landed.

3

Elizabeth sat on a blue chair
facing the window to write.

To her left, fish circled
below the surface
framed on the wall.

The black Underwood typewriter
settled on the table in front of her
was as heavy as an anchor.
Through cotton curtain mesh,
she studied shades of moss
on the blacksmith shop's
thatched roof jutting above
a hedge of purple lilacs next door
and listened for the clanging.

Laced light cast a fishnet shadow
on a white bay of paper
and keys to the alphabet.
She waited for it to catch the first word
then all of them thereafter.

Elizabeth Bishop House, Nova Scotia

Brass Ring

Old enough to still call it jogging,
I jogged past the carousel on Funtown Pier,
one of the few rides left standing
after Hurricane Sandy.
       Old enough to remember reaching
for the brass ring.
       What I didn't know then
was that what wave and wind
hadn't consumed of the past
would be swallowed by fire
before summer ended.

       No more whirling with the Wurlitzer
trailing scribbles of light
       No more gold-pole-pinned horses
galloping up and down in place.
       The wheel stopped spinning.
       Stars, floor to ceiling, snuffed out.

       In the beginning, ocean danced
with moon, and we swam in waves, broken
and made whole again.
       Then came a carousel of lights
with hand-painted horses
and a Wurlitzer organ
reeling alongside the water.
       In the beginning was the spinning,
simply to spin. To be alive and dizzy.
To watch the world whirl by.
And whirl with it. To be made tipsy.
       And then there was to reach.
The reaching. A pudgy hand. A brass ring.
And maybe a lucky grab, a free ride.

       But no more whirling with the Wurlitzer
trailing scribbles of light
       No more gold-pole-pinned horses

galloping up and down in place.
        The wheel stopped spinning.
        Stars, floor to ceiling, snuffed out.

                                    Seaside Heights, NJ

The Great Escape

It started at dusk with an abandoned car
in the Great Swamp. I was thirteen
and had never seen such a thing
as a rusted Chevy sunk hubcap-deep in the woods
and imprisoned by birch trees.
The passenger-side door hung open,
half unhinged and pockmarked with bullet holes.
No tires. Every window broken.
A single windshield-wiper's bent arm
hailed a tow truck that was never coming.
The front seat reached door to door
and there was a stick shift on the column
like my father's car but between the gas pedal
and clutch, a corroded orb of light in the floor.
To the right of the radio was a socket
for a cigarette lighter but no lighter,
and the glove compartment was empty.
Carved into the dashboard, the sum of a pair of initials
inside a jagged heart. Rusty springs coiled up
from the backseat's shredded upholstery.
As sun set, my head began to spin
with stories about high school sweethearts
parked after dark or runaways
who drove off-road for a secluded place
to spend the night. They never found the bodies.
They never find the bodies.
I have no better idea now than I did then
how long it takes a swamp to swallow a car
or bones for that matter. All I know is that night
I sat behind the wheel of a Chevy jailed in by trees
and sinking and started a car without any keys,
adjusted the rear-view mirror, checked my look,
checked the woods behind me for approaching deer
then pulled out of the forest as if from a green side-street,
cranked up the radio, and floored it for the open road.

Refuge

It is always the smooth-skinned
some people have to cut.
In a forest, the beech tree's sleek bark,
for instance. A pair of initials carved
inside a heart and dated.

Or on the news, that delicate boy
dragged into the woods. FAG
cut into his hairless chest.
As if love can be branded.

Always a proclamation, isn't it?
Someone leaving their mark.

I read a rabbi said that although God
was the same everywhere,
he had to go into the forest to find Him
because he wasn't.

I would trade a church
or a tropical resort
for a pair of hooded mergansers
on a pond in the woods.

The other day I stood up to my knees
in horsetails, once as tall as trees,
grazing a marsh.
I used to be so big, but now
I'm shrinking.

At the slightest touch, the pond shivered,
wrinkling the mirror.
A willow shook its hair out in the wind.

How is it this is not enough?

Back home, we have a name for everything
and a way we insist on being.
But there is a place in the woods
no matter what woods I'm in
where I have always been
even when I no longer am.

Memorial Day

   Harrison Street ripples red, white, and blue
from the American Legion to the cemetery
as the high school band threads a parade through town
playing *When the Saints Come Marching In.*
   Sunk in the backseat of a Thunderbird, our mayor,
one arm slung around the slumped shoulders
of a veteran in dress uniform propped beside him,
smiles solemnly, waves to the crowd.
   Between heroic speeches and Taps,
kids peck like chickens at Starbursts
and plastic-wrapped lollipops firemen toss
from a newly polished hook-and-ladder truck.
   We stand still and quiet on a green bridge
over the Delaware as seven soldiers wearing white helmets
and white gloves raise their rifles and fire three rounds
at the clouds.
   Poppies explode from an open hatch in the belly
of a single-engine plane soaring above the river
and spiral down a staircase of air.
   For some of us, their descent is personal,
a loved one overseas leafing through the wind;
others are simply distracted from the daily,
captivated by spectacle, or drawn in
for a moment, like me, to mourn
all lives cut short by war.
   While the airplane drones home
and the river carries off another armful of flowers,
we stop by the cemetery before heading back
to our front porch politics, seeded gardens,
dirty laundry, and all the other work left to be done.

Black Vulture

I go in through
the eyes first
or anus
rip the tongue
like a rubbery slug
from its grip
and hiss
as I unravel
intestines
link by link
like sausages
or plump
rosary beads
before I
suck the brain
from its shell.

Every morning
after reading the wind's
obituaries
I follow my nose
to feast
until full
at the paved buffet
of roadkill
then roost in a tree
within sight
of the highway
and sleep
without dreaming
not the murderer here
just part
of the cleanup crew.

Caulbearer

Same day I turned over my garden, iris bloomed
and my grandson was born in a balloon
because life has a way of humbling fiction.
Born *en caul*, not just his head hooded by a shroud of skin
but his entire body encapsulated in the amniotic sac
like a carnival goldfish in a plastic bag,
a bluish-gray being curled inside a gelatinous shell,
face smooshed flat against the curved membrane.
Medieval midwives used to press paper
against the sticky tissue to remove it from the body intact
then dry it out as an heirloom or talisman
for good fortune or for sale.
Back then, Isaac would be renowned as a caulbearer,
a truth-teller endowed with the gift of prophesy.
I don't know about that, but I do know the first night I held him
he cried with my daughter's eyes until it rained
then quieted as if he'd summoned the downpour
or, at least, foreseen it before falling asleep in my arms.

That Grackle

Catherine said the grackle flew up
from the lawn toward our feeder but
then fell to the walkway where I found it.
She saw the whole thing.
I have been watching birds all my life,
but I've never seen one let go of the sky
and drop dead mid-flight.
I have stumbled on a puddle of feathers
scattered in grass as if a bird exploded
or some quick claw or lightning talon
snagged, plucked, and un-stuffed
a sparrow or robin like a tiny pillow,
the winged thing distracted by seed
or worm underfoot. Certainly,
I have flattened into asphalt
my share of roadkill and witnessed
a single wing sticking straight up
from the street, giving passers-by the finger.
Every now and then I hear of dead starlings
in biblical numbers raining down
on a small town like a plague
or an omen of the apocalypse,
which feels a lot closer than not these days.
But that grackle dropped in our yard.
Close up, its iridescent black feathers
glistened blue and purple
like northern lights or an oil spill
on the long road of night, wings slack
at its sides, beak quieted, head turned
on an ear, as if listening to what earth
has to say, sleeping with its eyes wide open,
dreaming of soaring beyond the starry cage
of this world while I gauged its weight
in my hand then stroked the sleek,
feathered stiffness of rigor mortis set in.
I carried the carcass around back
and laid the shimmering body

to rest in our bamboo stand
where the annoyance it flew with
gathers evenings to roost and cackle
about where they have been.

Blue Heron

for Catherine

I was rubbing circles with my fingertips
around the small of her back
as if it were a prayer bowl
when a humming rose from inside
and a stone settled under forty years of water
floated to the surface like a flattened bubble
then skipped across the river ringing out her name
to the other side of the world
where it stepped from the current
ducked behind a tall curtain of reeds
and emerged a blue heron.

A Clown on a Cross on Third Street

There was a clown on a cross on a telephone pole across from a stump in the road, each of its sixty-three rings a reminder that a storm can, at any time, snap a tree like a toothpick in its fingertips.

Last winter black ice hurled Renee through her car windshield into a cornfield rounding a bend on the way home from a numbing polisci night class, and she wasn't found until the following morning.

That spring, Terry planted cosmos around the stump so when her daughter woke and came home from the hospital, she could watch the blossoms dance with passing traffic while she convalesced in a rocking chair on the porch.

Renee did come home and rock and watch flowers grow and listen to Top Soil rehearse next door. At first, she told her mother, the upright bass did something foggy, made her forget all about hospital bills,

but then the guitar stepped in, got her feet tapping again, and snappy lyrics made her want to rail against the health care system, march for socialized medicine, do something. She was sick of rocking in place on a porch.

Come Halloween, when the bass guitarist nailed a clown on a cross to the telephone pole in the road, Renee took it as a sign, had the drummer tattoo KICK BACK on her knuckles.

Then, while the band covered *Small Axe* and tipsy vampires in blue suits and high-heeled witches guzzled red wine with a splash of moonlight, Renee stepped down from her porch, over the cosmos, back into the street,

and behind the wheel again to the capitol city while trick-or-treaters packed in vans descended on Third Street from surrounding farmlands like locusts and demanded pillowcases full of candy.

Blue Note

Don't play what's there, play what's not there. ~Miles Davis

Sometimes, the moment is one long blue note
like the other day, before dark, as I walked by
a restored barn tucked in a corner of stone wall
still standing at the mouth of a cul-de-sac of
mock Tudors, a wind-rippled blue curtain
rushed from an open window where a loft
might be, as if the barn was breathing
and a trumpet, like the breath inside the breath,
as Kabir said of god, exhaled a watery blue moan
then sucked it back in as fast as a frog's tongue
or a pilot light gone out when it stopped playing.

Portal

for Joe Strasser

In bandanaed old dreads thick as bananas, Army boots, and paint-splattered overalls like a palette of himself, gravel grinding inside him in the sound of his voice, Joe ranted about charlatan artists and pig-pen galleries, corporate slaughterhouses, and curators *who couldn't tell a Pollack from a… Twombly was right,* he pointed to the sky, *If I had to do it over again, I would just do the paintings and never show them.* Then he rolled another tree trunk under a lean-to attached to an out-building in his backyard. After he covered the make-shift foundation with plywood, stacked and nailed discarded windows together for walls, windows he'd collected from friends doing renovations or leaning on garbage cans around town, he caulked and painted the frames dark forest green, then christened his new studio, *The Chicken Coop.*

Late nights, cooped up, kushed out, hotboxed, and psilocybin wired, Ornette Coleman knocking at the windows, nobody gets in or out while Joe stretches a bedsheet on the floor then lets loose the buzzing in his head like hornets from a paper nest of shredded, 60s LIFE magazine scraps and collages them in glued layers. He brushes over a decade of strata with bold stokes of white paint—*Where the bodies aren't, yet.* He swears ancient alien astronauts have traveled so far ahead of us that we've found traces of them in our past. Joe dips in and out of the bedsheet like a chicken hunched over night, pecking at stars. The only time he isn't ranting about Dada, The Kybalion, or the Doors of Perception is when he is looking hard into a work, so hard not only can he see the aliens coming, but he paints the way for them.

A Bird of Feathers

What if one morning out for a walk
a writer finds a bird's worth of feathers
like a puddle in the grass but no body,
no bones or blood even, nothing
but a black, white, and gray splash
as if a mockingbird smacked into earth
so hard it knocked its feathers off,
but the bird got up and walked away
or maybe when it hit, the body,
plucked at impact, left feathers behind,
passed through the ground like a ghost,
and popped out on the other side,
despite what Americans think,
not in China but in the Indian Ocean,
naked and unable to swim.
Or suppose, the instant before bird
and earth collided, bird disappeared
into the gilded cage of the past
or the drone-zone skies ahead
or an entirely different dimension,
naked in any case, its feathers
still stuck back in the grass.
Immobilized, unable to fly on their own,
and no longer pin-cushioned together
like dandelion seeds,
the feathers perch on the green fingertips
of a tightly trimmed lawn until a breeze
or a passerby flicks them away. What if
the writer who stops to inspect
feathers splattered on the ground
like a crime scene gathers them up,
brings them home to a table
by a desk near a window,
and pieces a bird back together
by connecting each feather to a word
until words assembled resemble
a mockingbird, not the whole bird,

of course, just enough to hear it sing?
It doesn't really sing though, does it?
At least not its own song,
and never one that tells the reader
where it's really gone.

John **Smith**'s poetry has appeared in journals such as *SmartishPace, Berfrois Journal, The Literary Review,* and *Spillway.* His work has been set to music by composer, Tina Davidson, and commissioned by New Jersey Audubon. His previous poetry collection is titled *Even That Indigo.* John lives in Frenchtown, NJ with his wife, the calligrapher and henna artist, Catherine Lent.